Collins

easy le

Multiplication and division

quick quizzes

Ages 7–9

Trevor Dixon

3 and 4 times tables

Draw a line from each multiplication to the correct answer.

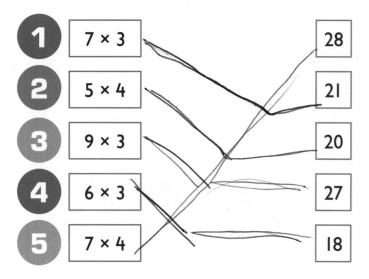

1	7 × 3
2	5 × 4
3	9 × 3
4	6 × 3
5	7 × 4

| 28 |
| 21 |
| 20 |
| 27 |
| 18 |

This is a ×3 function machine.

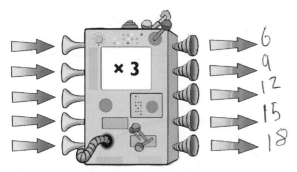

6
9
12
15
18

Write the missing numbers.

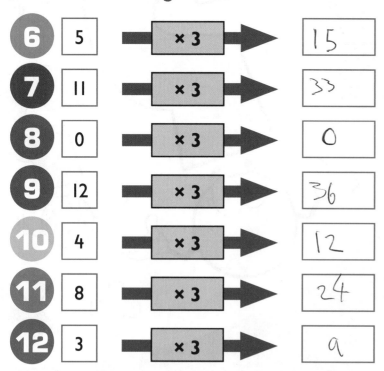

6	5	× 3	15
7	11	× 3	33
8	0	× 3	0
9	12	× 3	36
10	4	× 3	12
11	8	× 3	24
12	3	× 3	9

Colour your score

Dividing by 3 and 4

Circle the correct answers.

1   24 ÷ 3 =   6   7   (8)

2   32 ÷ 4 =   6   7   (8)

3   21 ÷ 3 =   6   (7)   8

4   24 ÷ 4 =   (6)   7   8

5   18 ÷ 3 =   (6)   7   8

6   28 ÷ 4 =   6   (7)   8

If you know 3 × 5, then you know 15 ÷ 3.

Write the missing number.

7 | 0 | ÷   4   =   0

8   30   ÷ | 10 | =   3

9 | 4 | ÷   3   =   12

10   20   ÷ | 4 | =   5

11 | 1.5 | ÷   3   =   4

12   15   ÷ | 1 | =   5

13 | 3 | ÷   4   =   12

14   24   ÷ | ?! | =   6

15 | 3 | ÷   3   =   9

Colour your score

8 times table

Circle the correct answers.

1   4 × 8 =   **30**   **32**   **34**

2   6 × 8 =   **48**   **50**   **52**

3   12 × 8 =   **92**   **94**   **96**

4   7 × 8 =   **54**   **56**   **58**

5   9 × 8 =   **68**   **70**   **72**

> Try multiplying by 4 and then doubling the answer.

This is a ×8 function machine.

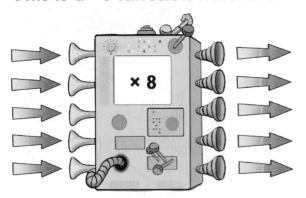

×8

Write the missing numbers.

6 | 5 | → **× 8** → | |

7 | | → **× 8** → | 88 |

8 | 0 | → **× 8** → | |

9 | | → **× 8** → | 24 |

10 | 8 | → **× 8** → | |

11 | | → **× 8** → | 8 |

12 | 10 | → **× 8** → | |

Colour your score

12
11
10
9
8
7
6
5
4
3
2
1

Dividing by 8

Fill in in the missing numbers.

1   16   ÷   8   =   [ ]

2   [ ]   ÷   8   =   5

3   24   ÷   8   =   [ ]

4   [ ]   ÷   8   =   11

5   32   ÷   8   =   [ ]

6   [ ]   ÷   8   =   7

7   72   ÷   8   =   [ ]

8   [ ]   ÷   8   =   4

9   64   ÷   8   =   [ ]

10   [ ]   ÷   8   =   12

Write <, > or = in each box.

11   88   ÷   8   [ ]   9

12   16   ÷   8   [ ]   4

13   48   ÷   8   [ ]   6

14   56   ÷   8   [ ]   8

15   72   ÷   8   [ ]   7

Try dividing by four and then halving the answer.

Colour your score

15 14 13 12 11 10 9 8 7 6 5 4 3 2 1

Using number facts

Write true or false for each number sentence.

1 $3 \times 8 = 6 \times 4$ _____

2 $6 \times 8 = 12 \times 4$ _____

3 $3 \times 8 = 9 \times 4$ _____

4 $27 \div 3 = 36 \div 4$ _____

5 $4 \times 3 = 88 \div 8$ _____

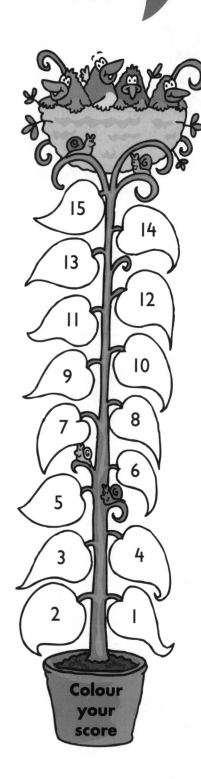

Use the multiplication and division facts you know.

Write <, > or = in each box.

6 4×8 ☐ 9×3

7 7×3 ☐ 6×4

8 $64 \div 8$ ☐ $32 \div 8$

9 2×8 ☐ 4×4

10 $72 \div 8$ ☐ $48 \div 4$

Fill in the missing numbers.

11 ☐ $\times \ 8 \ = \ 96$

12 $8 \ \times$ ☐ $= \ 64$

13 ☐ $\div \ 8 \ = \ 6$

14 $36 \ \div$ ☐ $= \ 12$

15 ☐ $\div \ 4 \ = \ 9$

Colour your score

More using number facts

Fill in the missing numbers.

1   20   ×   ☐   =   5

2   9   ×   ☐   =   72

3   27   ÷   ☐   =   9

4   7   ×   ☐   =   28

5   33   ÷   ☐   =   11

Circle the number that is in:

6   the 3 **and** 4 times tables.   9   12   16

7   the 3 **and** 5 times tables.   21   25   30

8   the 4 **and** 8 times tables.   36   44   48

9   the 3 **and** 4 times tables.   24   27   32

Write three one-digit numbers to complete each number sentence.

10   ☐ × ☐ × ☐ = 24

11   ☐ × ☐ × ☐ = 36

12   ☐ × ☐ × ☐ = 40

How quickly can you answer these questions?

12
11
10
9
8
7
6
5
4
3
1
2

Colour your score

Mental multiplication

Write the answers.

1   13   ×   5   =

2   17   ×   3   =

3   15   ×   4   =

4   16   ×   5   =

5   14   ×   3   =

6   23   ×   4   =

7   24   ×   5   =

8   13   ×   8   =

9   21   ×   5   =

10   34   ×   2   =

11   13   ×   4   =

12   21   ×   8   =

13   18   ×   5   =

14   23   ×   3   =

15   18   ×   4   =

You could partition the two-digit number, e.g.
24×4
$= (20 \times 4) + (4 \times 4)$
$= 80 + 16$
$= 96$

Colour your score

Written multiplication

Complete each multiplication.

1
```
    3  2
×      4
―――――――
```

2
```
    3  1
×      5
―――――――
```

3
```
    5  3
×      8
―――――――
```

4
```
    8  5
×      3
―――――――
```

5
```
    6  7
×      4
―――――――
```

6
```
    8  5
×      5
―――――――
```

7
```
    6  4
×      8
―――――――
```

8
```
    4  5
×      3
―――――――
```

9
```
    5  6
×      4
―――――――
```

10
```
    7  4
×      8
―――――――
```

11
```
    8  3
×      5
―――――――
```

12
```
    6  8
×      4
―――――――
```

13
```
    9  6
×      4
―――――――
```

14
```
    5  8
×      8
―――――――
```

Remember to multiply the ones first.

Colour your score

Written division

Complete these divisions.

Remember to work from left to right.

1   4) 8 4   2 1

2   3) 6 3   2 1

3   2) 6 8   3 4

4   3) 5²4

5   4) 7³6   1

6   4) 5 6

7   5) 6 5

8   5) 7 0

9   2) 7 4

10   4) 9 2

11   3) 7 2

12   5) 9 0

13   2) 8 8

14   4) 9 6

15   5) 8 5

Colour your score

15 14 13 12 11 10 9 8 7 6 5 4 3 2 1

What number?

Write the answers.

1 I multiply a number by 5. The answer is 35.

What number did I multiply? ☐

2 I divide a number by 4. The answer is 8.

What number did I divide? ☐

3 I divide 24 by a number. The answer is 8.

What number did I divide by? ☐

4 I multiply 8 by a number. The answer is 40.

What number did I multiply by? ☐

5 I multiply a number by 3. The answer is 27.

What number did I multiply? ☐

6 I divide 28 by a number. The answer is 4.

What number did I divide by? ☐

7 I multiply 3 by a number. The answer is 21.

What number did I multiply by? ☐

8 I multiply a number by 4. The answer is 48.

What number did I multiply? ☐

9 I divide a number by 6. The answer is 6.

What number did I divide? ☐

10 I divide 45 by a number. The answer is 5.

What number did I divide by? ☐

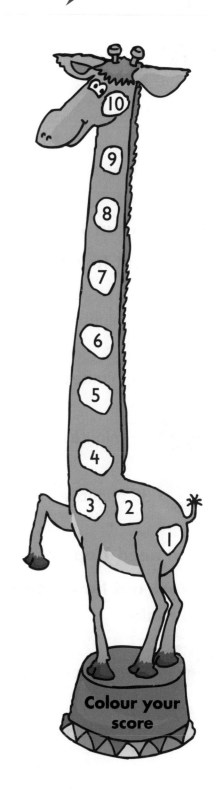

Write a number sentence if you need to.

Colour your score

11

Scaling problems

Zak works for 2 hours and completes 10 metres of fencing.

Work out how many metres of fencing Zak could complete in:

Work out how many times bigger or smaller the amounts have become.

1 6 hours  m

2 10 hours  m

3 1 hour  m

4 3 hours  m

Nia can run 3 kilometres in 5 minutes.

Work out how far she could run in:

5 15 minutes  km

6 20 minutes  km

7 $2\frac{1}{2}$ minutes  km

8 30 minutes  km

You need 7 apples to make 10 small pies.

Work out how many apples you need to make:

9 20 small pies  apples

10 100 small pies  apples

Colour your score

More scaling problems

Jo draws a plan of her kitchen.

On the plan, I cm means 10 cm in real life.

Work out the real life measurements for these lengths:

Use your multiplication facts to work out the answers.

1 3 cm ➡ [ ] cm

2 6 cm ➡ [ ] cm

3 10 cm ➡ [ ] cm

4 2.5 cm ➡ [ ] cm

5 5.5 cm ➡ [ ] cm

A sandwich shop has different choices of bread and fillings.

Work out how many different combinations there are for:

6 3 types of bread and 4 fillings ➡ [ ]

7 4 types of bread and 5 fillings ➡ [ ]

8 4 types of bread and 8 fillings ➡ [ ]

9 3 types of bread and 5 fillings ➡ [ ]

10 4 types of bread and 10 fillings ➡ [ ]

Colour your score

13

Multiplication facts

Write the answers.

1 5 × 8 = 40

2 4 × 12 = 48

3 5 × 9 = 36

4 7 × 7 = 49

5 7 × 6 = 42

6 12 × 12 =

7 9 × 9 =

8 12 × 7 =

9 12 × 9 =

10 9 × 7 =

If you don't know a fact, work from a fact you do know or see if you can reverse it.

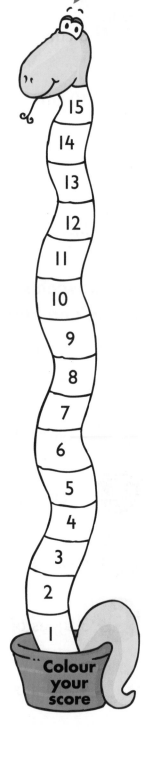

Complete this table for a ×7 function machine.

× 7	
Number in	**Number out**
12	
5	
9	
6	
8	

11   **12**   **13**   **14**   **15**

Colour your score

Missing numbers

Fill in the missing numbers.

Decide whether to multiply or divide to find the missing number.

1 ☐ × 6 = 48

2 7 × ☐ = 35

3 42 ÷ ☐ = 6

4 ☐ × 12 = 108

5 84 ÷ 7 = ☐

6 9 × ☐ = 54

7 ☐ × 9 = 63

8 36 ÷ ☐ = 9

9 56 ÷ 7 = ☐

10 ☐ ÷ 12 = 8

11 ☐ × 7 = 35

12 72 ÷ ☐ = 6

13 ☐ ÷ 7 = 4

14 ☐ × 9 = 72

15 77 ÷ ☐ = 7

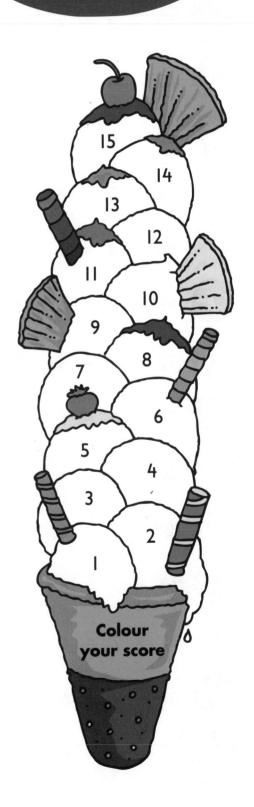

Colour your score

Division facts

All these division facts have an answer of 6, 7, 9 or 12.

Circle the correct answer for each fact.

1   54 ÷ 6 =   **6**   **7**   **9**   **12**

2   48 ÷ 8 =   **6**   **7**   **9**   **12**

3   42 ÷ 6 =   **6**   **7**   **9**   **12**

4   48 ÷ 4 =   **6**   **7**   **9**   **12**

5   72 ÷ 8 =   **6**   **7**   **9**   **12**

6   96 ÷ 8 =   **6**   **7**   **9**   **12**

7   49 ÷ 7 =   **6**   **7**   **9**   **12**

8   72 ÷ 12 =   **6**   **7**   **9**   **12**

9   56 ÷ 8 =   **6**   **7**   **9**   **12**

10   60 ÷ 5 =   **6**   **7**   **9**   **12**

11   108 ÷ 9 =   **6**   **7**   **9**   **12**

12   63 ÷ 7 =   **6**   **7**   **9**   **12**

13   42 ÷ 7 =   **6**   **7**   **9**   **12**

14   81 ÷ 9 =   **6**   **7**   **9**   **12**

15   84 ÷ 12 =   **6**   **7**   **9**   **12**

You can solve 72 ÷ 6 by thinking, 'How many sixes make seventy-two?'

Colour your score

15
14
13
12
11
10
9
8
7
6
5
4
3
2
1

More missing numbers

Write the missing numbers.

1 ☐ ÷ 5 = 9

2 ☐ ÷ 9 = 7

3 48 ÷ ☐ = 12

4 ☐ ÷ 6 = 7

5 ☐ ÷ 9 = 4

6 54 ÷ ☐ = 6

7 ☐ ÷ 7 = 7

8 ☐ ÷ 9 = 12

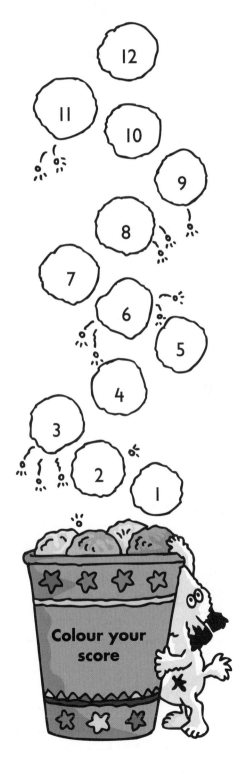

Colour your score

Write the answers.

9 I divide a number by 7. The answer is 12.

What number did I divide? ☐

10 I multiply a number by 11. The answer is 110.

What number did I multiply? ☐

11 I divide 72 by a number. The answer is 12.

What number did I divide by? ☐

12 I multiply a number by itself. The number is 81.

What number did I multiply? ☐

Using place value

Write the missing numbers and answers.

1 $55 \times 3 = (50 \times 3) + (5 \times 3)$

$= 150 +$ [ ] $=$ [ ]

Partition the two-digit number before multiplying. Then add the products.

2 $26 \times 4 = (20 \times 4) + (6 \times 4)$

$= 80 +$ [ ] $=$ [ ]

3 $43 \times 5 = (40 \times 5) + (3 \times 5)$

$= 200 +$ [ ] $=$ [ ]

4 $47 \times 3 = (40 \times 3) + (7 \times 3)$

$=$ [ ] $+$ [ ] $=$ [ ]

5 $52 \times 5 = (50 \times 5) + (2 \times 5)$

$=$ [ ] $+$ [ ] $=$ [ ]

6 $54 \times 4 = (50 \times 4) + (4 \times 4)$

$=$ [ ] $+$ [ ] $=$ [ ]

7 $45 \times 6 = ($ [ ] $\times 6) + ($ [ ] $\times 6)$

$=$ [ ] $+$ [ ] $=$ [ ]

8 $24 \times 9 = ($ [ ] $\times 9) + ($ [ ] $\times 9)$

$=$ [ ] $+$ [ ] $=$ [ ]

9 $35 \times 8 = ($ [ ] $\times 8) + ($ [ ] $\times 8)$

$=$ [ ] $+$ [ ] $=$ [ ]

10 $54 \times 3 = ($ [ ] $\times 3) + ($ [ ] $\times 3)$

$=$ [ ] $+$ [ ] $=$ [ ]

Colour your score

10 9 8 7 6 5 4 3 2 1

Using known facts

Fill in the missing numbers.

1   5 × 4 = [ ] , so 50 × 4 = [ ]

2   3 × 6 = [ ] , so 3 × 60 = [ ]

3   3 × 8 = [ ] , so 30 × 8 = [ ]

4   6 × 6 = [ ] , so 6 × 60 = [ ]

5   7 × 5 = [ ] , so 70 × 5 = [ ]

6   7 × 7 = [ ] , so 700 × 7 = [ ]

7   9 × 6 = [ ] , so 9 × 600 = [ ]

8   6 × 7 = [ ] , so 600 × 7 = [ ]

9   8 × 7 = [ ] , so 8 × 700 = [ ]

10   9 × 9 = [ ] , so 900 × 9 = [ ]

Write a tick if the answer is 2400.
Write a cross if it is not.

11   30   ×   8   [ ]

12   4   ×   600   [ ]

13   60   ×   4   [ ]

14   2   ×   1200   [ ]

15   800   ×   3   [ ]

The first multiplication fact helps with the second one.

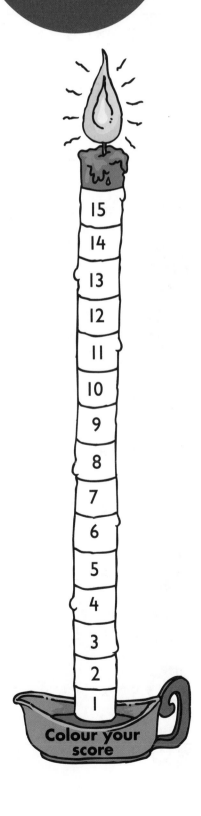

15
14
13
12
11
10
9
8
7
6
5
4
3
2
1

Colour your score

19

Multiplying three numbers

Write the answers.

1 3 × 2 × 5 =

2 2 × 4 × 3 =

3 2 × 3 × 3 =

4 1 × 8 × 6 =

5 5 × 2 × 6 =

6 2 × 3 × 9 =

7 4 × 7 × 0 =

8 5 × 4 × 5 =

9 3 × 4 × 5 =

10 6 × 2 × 6 =

11 4 × 12 × 2 =

12 7 × 3 × 4 =

13 6 × 5 × 4 =

14 9 × 4 × 2 =

15 3 × 5 × 6 =

Remember, you can multiply the three numbers in any order!

Colour your score

20

Factor pairs

Multiply the two numbers and write the answer. Then find another factor pair with the same product.
Do not use the number 1.

1 3 and 4 is a factor pair of ☐

Another factor pair is ☐ and ☐

2 4 and 5 is a factor pair of ☐

Another factor pair is ☐ and ☐

3 3 and 8 is a factor pair of ☐

Another factor pair is ☐ and ☐

4 2 and 14 are a factor pair of ☐

Another factor pair is ☐ and ☐

5 3 and 12 are a factor pair of ☐

Another factor pair is ☐ and ☐

Factor pairs are pairs of numbers that multiply to make a particular number.

Fill in the matching coloured boxes to show all the factor pairs.

6 Factor pairs of 18:

| 1 | | | | | 18 |

7 Factor pairs of 30:

| 1 | | | | | | 30 |

8 Factor pairs of 27:

| 1 | | | |

Colour your score

Commutativity

Fill in the missing numbers.

1 $6 \times 3 = \boxed{} = 3 \times \boxed{}$

2 $8 \times 4 = \boxed{} = \boxed{} \times 8$

3 $4 \times \boxed{} = \boxed{} = 9 \times 4$

4 $\boxed{} \times 7 = \boxed{} = 7 \times 6$

5 $4 \times 12 = \boxed{} = 12 \times \boxed{}$

6 $6 \times 8 = \boxed{} = \boxed{} \times 6$

7 $9 \times \boxed{} = \boxed{} = 6 \times 9$

8 $\boxed{} \times 7 = \boxed{} = 7 \times 8$

9 $8 \times 9 = \boxed{} = 9 \times \boxed{}$

10 $6 \times 12 = \boxed{} = \boxed{} \times 6$

11 $8 \times \boxed{} = \boxed{} = 11 \times 8$

12 $\boxed{} \times 7 = \boxed{} = 7 \times 12$

13 $11 \times 9 = \boxed{} = 9 \times \boxed{}$

14 $12 \times 11 = \boxed{} = \boxed{} \times 12$

15 $9 \times \boxed{} = \boxed{} = 12 \times 9$

15
14
13
12
11
10
9
8
7
6
5
4
3
2
1

Colour your score

Multiplying 2-digit numbers

Complete the multiplications.

1
```
   2 3
×    4
   9 2
  1
```

2
```
   5 3
×    5
 2 6 5
  1
```

3
```
   3 3
×    6
 1 9 8
  1
```

4
```
   4 6
×    8
 3 6 8
    4
```

5
```
   5 3
×    9
 4 7 7
```

6
```
   6 2
×    8
 4 9 6
```

7
```
   7 3
×    7
 5 1 1
```

8
```
   5 2
×    9
 4 6 8
```

9
```
   6 5
×    8
 5 2 0
```

10
```
   4 8
×    7
 3 3 6
```

11
```
   7 2
×    9
 6 4 8
```

12
```
   8 4
×    6
 5 0 4
```

13
```
   9 5
×    8
 7 6 0
```

14
```
   6 7
×    9
 6 0 3
```

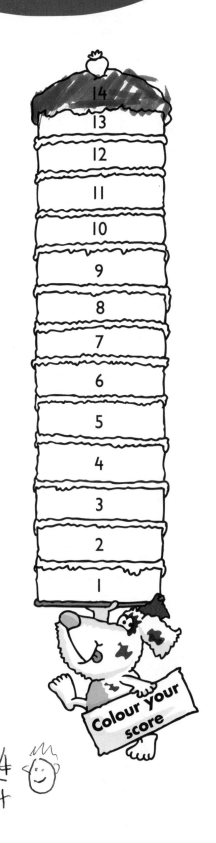

Colour your score

$\frac{14}{14}$

Missing digits

Fill in the missing numbers.

1

```
    4  □
  ×    4
  -------
  1  8  4
```
2

6

```
  □    7
  ×    8
  -------
  2  1  6
```
5

Look at the product of the ones!

2

```
  □    5
  ×    5
  -------
  1  7  5
```
2

7

```
    4  □
  ×    5
  -------
  2  3  5
```
3

3

```
  □    8
  ×    8
  -------
  3  0  4
```
6

8

```
  □    5
  ×    6
  -------
  4  5  0
```
3

4

```
    4  □
  ×    6
  -------
  2  8  2
```
4

9

```
  □    2
  ×    8
  -------
  7  3  6
```
1

5

```
    6  □
  ×    6
  -------
  4  1  4
```
5

10

```
    2  □
  ×    9
  -------
  2  3  4
```
5

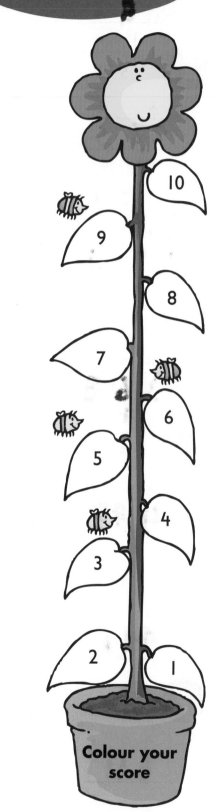

10
9
8
7
6
5
4
3
2
1

Colour your score

24

Multiplying 3-digit numbers

Write the answers.

1
```
    4 1 7
  ×     4
  ───────
```

2
```
    3 7 2
  ×     5
  ───────
```

3
```
    7 4 3
  ×     3
  ───────
```

4
```
    5 6 2
  ×     2
  ───────
```

5
```
    6 3 5
  ×     8
  ───────
```

6
```
    8 2 0
  ×     6
  ───────
```

7
```
    9 6 7
  ×     5
  ───────
```

8
```
    6 0 8
  ×     8
  ───────
```

9
```
    8 1 9
  ×     9
  ───────
```

10
```
    2 8 6
  ×     7
  ───────
```

11
```
    4 8 2
  ×     6
  ───────
```

12
```
    8 8 2
  ×     4
  ───────
```

Do not forget to add any carried numbers.

Colour your score

25

More missing digits

Write the missing number.

1

```
  4 □ 5
×     5
───────
2 1 7 5
  1   2
```

6

```
  4 □ 6
×     5
───────
2 1 3 0
  1   3
```

Work through the calculation and think what the missing number could be.

2

```
  6 4 □
×     4
───────
2 5 8 4
  1   2
```

7

```
  5 7 □
×     7
───────
4 0 1 1
  5   2
```

3

```
  5 6 □
×     3
───────
1 7 0 7
  2   2
```

8

```
  5 □ 3
×     3
───────
1 7 7 9
    2
```

4

```
  4 □ 2
×     4
───────
1 7 2 8
  1
```

9

```
  6 5 □
×     6
───────
3 9 4 2
  3   4
```

5

```
  1 3 □
×     6
───────
  8 1 6
    2   3
```

10

```
  4 □ 9
×     7
───────
3 2 1 3
  4   6
```

Colour your score

26

Problem-solving

A sack of potatoes has a mass of 45 kg.

Work out the total mass of:

1 4 sacks  ☐ kg

2 5 sacks  ☐ kg

3 8 sacks  ☐ kg

Karen cycles 35 km every day.

Work out how far she cycles in:

4 7 days  ☐ km

5 4 days ☐ km

6 8 days ☐ km

A ticket for a concert costs £28.

7 What is the cost of 4 tickets?

£ ☐

8 Josh buys 5 tickets.
How much will he have left from £150?

£ ☐

9 Kira wants 9 tickets. She has £188.
How much more money does she need?

£ ☐

10 Samir has ten £20 notes. He buys 6 tickets.
How much money does he have left?

£ ☐

Use multiplication to solve these problems.

Colour your score

More problem-solving

There are **96** cartons of orange juice that need packing.

How many boxes are needed if there are:

1 3 cartons in a box? ➡️ [   ] boxes

2 6 cartons in a box? ➡️ [   ] boxes

3 8 cartons in box? ➡️ [   ] boxes

Sharon plays a computer game. She scores **75** points at each level.

Work out how many points she scores if she completes:

4 5 levels ➡️ [   ] points

5 8 levels ➡️ [   ] points

6 7 levels ➡️ [   ] points

An adult train ticket costs **£17** and a child ticket costs **£9**.

7 What is the cost of 2 adult tickets and 3 child tickets?

£ [   ]

8 Dev spends £53 on tickets.
He buys one adult ticket.
How many child tickets did he buy?

[   ] child tickets

Look for clues to help you decide whether to multiply or divide.

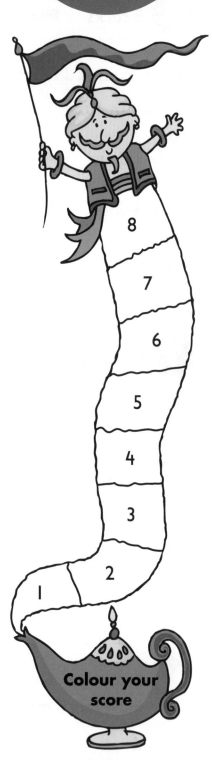

8
7
6
5
4
3
2
1

Colour your score

Partitioning

Write the missing numbers and the answers.

1 45 × 3 = (40 × 3) + (5 × ☐) = ☐

2 35 × 4 = (30 × 4) + (☐ × 4) = ☐

3 53 × 5 = (50 × ☐) + (3 × 5) = ☐

4 62 × 6 = (☐ × 6) + (2 × 6) = ☐

5 73 × 8 = (70 × 8) + (3 × ☐) = ☐

6 29 × 6 = (20 × 6) + (☐ × 6) = ☐

7 82 × 3 = (80 × ☐) + (2 × 3) = ☐

8 57 × 8 = (☐ × 8) + (7 × 8) = ☐

9 81 × 9 = (80 × 9) + (1 × ☐) = ☐

10 64 × 6 = (60 × 6) + (☐ × 6) = ☐

11 72 × 9 = (70 × ☐) + (2 × 9) = ☐

12 39 × 7 = (☐ × 7) + (9 × 7) = ☐

13 86 × 6 = (80 × 6) + (6 × ☐) = ☐

14 95 × 4 = (90 × 4) + (☐ × 4) = ☐

15 68 × 9 = (60 × ☐) + (8 × 9) = ☐

Partition the two-digit number before you multiply.

Colour your score

29

Recipes

These are the ingredients needed for 2 smoothies:

8 strawberries	3 tablespoons sugar
100 ml milk	6 crushed ice cubes
120 ml yoghurt	

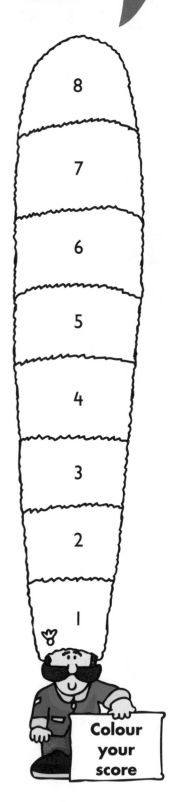

How many times have the numbers grown? Multiply by that number.

1 If you want to use 400 ml of milk, how much yoghurt do you need? ⬚ ml

2 How many smoothies can you make with 40 strawberries? ⬚ smoothies

3 How many strawberries do you need to make 6 smoothies? ⬚ strawberries

This is a list of ingredients needed to make 15 brownies:

400 g chocolate	4 eggs
250 g butter	150 g flour
300 g sugar	

4 How many brownies can you make with 800 g chocolate? ⬚ brownies

5 How many eggs do you need to make 30 brownies? ⬚ eggs

6 How much sugar do you need to make 60 brownies? ⬚ g

7 How many brownies can you make with 50 g of flour? ⬚ brownies

8 How many brownies can you make with 12 eggs? ⬚ brownies

Colour your score

How much?

Write the answers.

1 6 mushrooms have a mass of 90 g.
What is the mass of 2 mushrooms?

[ ] g

2 3 pizzas cost £9.
How much do 2 pizzas cost? £ [ ]

3 4 benches can seat 24 children.
How many children can sit on 3 benches?

[ ] children

4 2 tomatoes cost 30 p.
How much do 6 tomatoes cost? [ ] p

5 4 books cost £16.
How much do 3 books cost? £ [ ]

6 Ben can walk 12 km in 2 hours.
How far can he walk in 3 hours? [ ] km

7 Tom earns £16 for 2 hours' work.
How much will he earn in 5 hours? £ [ ]

8 4 cans of drink cost £2.
How much do 5 cans cost? £ [ ]

9 3 oranges cost £1.20.
How much do 2 oranges cost? [ ] p

10 450 ml of juice is enough for 3 drinks.
How much juice is needed for 5 drinks?

[ ] ml

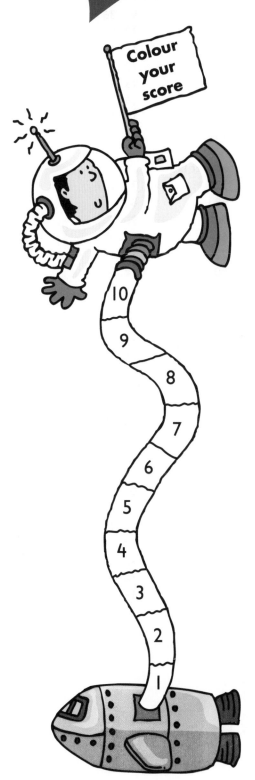

Start by finding the value, mass or cost of one.

Colour your score

10
9
8
7
6
5
4
3
2
1

Answers

3 and 4 times tables
1. 21
2. 20
3. 27
4. 18
5. 28
6. 15
7. 33
8. 0
9. 36
10. 12
11. 24
12. 9

Dividing by 3 and 4
1. 8
2. 8
3. 7
4. 6
5. 6
6. 7
7. 0
8. 10
9. 36
10. 4
11. 12
12. 3
13. 48
14. 4
15. 27

8 times table
1. 32
2. 48
3. 96
4. 56
5. 72
6. 40
7. 11
8. 0
9. 3
10. 64
11. 1
12. 80

Dividing by 8
1. 2
2. 40
3. 3
4. 88
5. 4
6. 56
7. 9
8. 32
9. 8
10. 96
11. >
12. <
13. =
14. <
15. >

Using number facts
1. True
2. True
3. False
4. True
5. False
6. >
7. <
8. >
9. =
10. <
11. 12
12. 8
13. 48
14. 3
15. 36

More using number facts
1. 4
2. 8
3. 3
4. 4
5. 3

6. 12
7. 30
8. 48
9. 24

There is a number of possible answers for questions 10–12.
10. Three numbers that multiply to 24, e.g. 2 × 3 × 4 or 2 × 2 × 6
11. Three numbers that multiply to 36, e.g. 2 × 3 × 6 or 3 × 3 × 4
12. Three numbers that multiply to 40, e.g. 2 × 4 × 5 or 2 × 2 × 10

Mental multiplication
1. 65
2. 51
3. 60
4. 80
5. 42
6. 92
7. 120
8. 104
9. 105
10. 68
11. 52
12. 168
13. 90
14. 69
15. 72

Written multiplication
1. 128
2. 155
3. 424
4. 255
5. 268
6. 425
7. 512
8. 135
9. 224
10. 592
11. 415
12. 272
13. 384
14. 464

Written division
1. 21
2. 21
3. 34
4. 18
5. 19
6. 14
7. 13
8. 14
9. 37
10. 23
11. 24
12. 18
13. 44
14. 24
15. 17

What number?
1. 7
2. 32
3. 3
4. 5
5. 9
6. 7
7. 7
8. 12
9. 36
10. 9

Scaling problems
1. 30 m
2. 50 m
3. 5 m
4. 15 m

5. 9 km
6. 12 km
7. $1\frac{1}{2}$ km
8. 18 km
9. 14 apples
10. 70 apples

More scaling problems
1. 30 cm
2. 60 cm
3. 100 cm
4. 25 cm
5. 55 cm
6. 12
7. 20
8. 32
9. 15
10. 40

Multiplication facts
1. 40
2. 48
3. 45
4. 49
5. 42
6. 144
7. 81
8. 84
9. 108
10. 63
11. 84
12. 35
13. 63
14. 42
15. 56

Missing numbers
1. 8
2. 5
3. 7
4. 9
5. 12
6. 6
7. 7
8. 4
9. 8
10. 96
11. 5
12. 12
13. 28
14. 8
15. 11

Division facts
1. 9
2. 6
3. 7
4. 12
5. 9
6. 12
7. 7
8. 6
9. 7
10. 12
11. 12
12. 9
13. 6
14. 9
15. 7

More missing numbers
1. 45
2. 63
3. 4
4. 42
5. 36
6. 9
7. 49
8. 108
9. 84
10. 10
11. 6
12. 9

Using place value
1. 15, 165
2. 24, 104